MW00560463

NORTH TO WEST
THE BEST OF MODERN CHICAGOLAND RAIL

JAMES KEATS JR. AND DAVID ZEMAN

AMERICA
THROUGH TIME®
ADDING COLOR TO AMERICAN HISTORY

Union Pacific 1948, an EMD SD40N, pilots a grain train from the Harvard Subdivision towards Proviso Yard while passing Howard Ave. in Des Plaines, Illinois, in a heavy snow storm. [*David Zeman*]

America Through Time is an imprint of Fonthill Media LLC
www.through-time.com
office@through-time.com

Published by Arcadia Publishing by arrangement with Fonthill Media LLC
For all general information, please contact Arcadia Publishing:
Telephone: 843-853-2070
Fax: 843-853-0044
E-mail: sales@arcadiapublishing.com
For customer service and orders:
Toll-Free 1-888-313-2665

www.arcadiapublishing.com

First published 2021

Copyright © James Keats Jr. and David Zeman 2021

ISBN 978-1-63499-343-2

All rights reserved. No part of this publication may be reproduced, stored
in a retrieval system or transmitted in any form or by any means, electronic,
mechanical, photocopying, recording or otherwise, without prior permission in
writing from Fonthill Media LLC

Typeset in Gotham Book
Printed and bound in England

CONTENTS

ACKNOWLEDGMENTS

There are many thanks to give for contributions to the railroad community and for the photographs showcased throughout this book. Firstly, thanks go out to David Dupuis, Kyle Krinninger, and James H. Lewnard for their photo contributions to the various chapters. We especially appreciate Kyle Krinninger who created the maps of each railroad line. Also, many thanks go to the railroad employees keeping America and the world moving night and day during the COVID-19 crisis and all the years previous to the pandemic. More thanks go out to all the Chicagoland photographers and railfans, who assist those around them in documenting trains across the area. Finally, the biggest thank you goes out to the many Illinois Railway Museum volunteers. Their tireless efforts, all on voluntary time, to preserve the railroad history of Chicagoland and the entire country sits unparalleled to any other organization. Chicago is a great city, with great people making their mark on documentation, preservation, and photography, and a massive thank you goes out to everyone in and around Chicago who helped make this book possible in any way.

COVER IMAGES

Front Cover: It is common for Metra trains to have two locomotives for power. In this case, an outbound Milwaukee District North train passes Rondout Tower with METX 123, an EMD F40PH, leading a former-Amtrak EMD F59PHI. [*David Zeman*]

Back Cover: UPY 709, a classic EMD GP15 locomotive, leads a sister GP15 with a local freight to Troy Grove, Illinois. The local is seen here diverting off the Geneva Subdivision at Dekalb, Illinois, and past the very popular Chicago and North Western coaling tower. This tower has sat over the Geneva Subdivision for 100+ years, serving as a constant reminder to the CNW's steam filled past. [*James Keats Jr.*]

As seen from the end of another train, St. Louis-San Francisco Railway 1630 passes by Johnson Siding on the museum's mainline with the coach train consisting of Pullman heavyweight passenger cars. [*David Zeman*]

INTRODUCTION

Chicago, Illinois. One of America's largest cities, biggest industrial hubs, and truly the definition of a city built around the railroad. Chicago has always been one of the railroad capitals of the United States, with some saying it holds the title unmatched. Dating far back into the 1800s, it has been a critical location for transportation of people and the goods needed to build the country. Stockyards and rail yards made up much of the land at the start of the twentieth century, with the city skyrises building in the background. Since then, railroad companies have always been driven to find the best route which would generate the most business. With various mainlines spanning cross country coming in and out of the city, a person cannot travel far in Chicago without running into train tracks. Many have recalled the rich history of railroads such as the Illinois Central, Pennsylvania Railroad, New York Central, and others spanning from Chicago to the south and east, but what about the railroads going to the north and the west?

The routes of the former Chicago & North Western Railroad encompass a largely undocumented region on film and paper alike in recent times. The North and West suburbs of Chicagoland hold gems of railroading that many do not even know about. From the cross-country lifelines of the Union Pacific, to small shortline railroads working industrial parks and grain elevators, Northern Illinois and Southern Wisconsin have some of the very best railroads and shots from around the world. Generations of photographers have documented the history of Chicagoland railroads. Each and every photographer has their own unique take on Chicagoland, all slightly different, and equally astonishing.

This book focuses on ten specific railroad lines coming from Chicago, as well as a railroad museum and miscellaneous train operations that work smaller areas in between subdivisions. What is covered geographically extends to approximately an 85-mile radius from Chicago's center in between the Union Pacific Geneva Subdivision which runs west to Iowa from Chicago and the UP Kenosha Subdivision which runs north to Milwaukee, Wisconsin. In addition to these two lines, Union Pacific's Milwaukee, Harvard, and Belvidere Subdivisions are also represented. In terms of other railroads, Canadian Pacific's Chicago/ Elgin and C&M Subdivisions are explored as well as Canadian National's Waukesha and Leithton Subdivisions. Lastly, the Metra and Wisconsin and Southern Railroad's Fox Lake Subdivisions are discussed. Highlights of five years of railroad photography, also known as "railfanning," make up the images taken by five different photographers.

Chicagoland is a beginning of many multi-generational lifelines to the west and north. Remnants of past railroads such as interlocking towers, vintage signals, old-fashioned depots, and coaling towers can be seen, reminding photographers of past times. For railroad lines running to the West Coast or into Canada, Chicago is the starting point for many of them. Moving people and goods is essential to the infrastructure of the United States, and the railroads are needed to keep everything going. As a central freight hub in the U.S., Chicago has always been a critical geographical location for passenger and freight service by rail.

Railroads such as Union Pacific, Canadian National, Canadian Pacific, Metra, Amtrak, and many more keep people and goods moving and attract railfans and photographers from all over the country. Since 2016, the railroading scene in Chicagoland and the entire United States has changed a lot. New diesel locomotives have come in and replaced older engines, leaving much evidence of previous railroad companies only to history. For example, the Canadian National Railway had undoubtedly the most interesting locomotive roster until approximately 2019. A mix of old British Columbia Rail GE C40-8 "Barn" engines, leased engines from other companies, and EMD standard cab locomotives were commonly seen leading trains in past years, but new GE Evolution Series locomotives have replaced them. The UP Harvard Subdivision required an EMD SD40N leader because of cab signal requirements until late 2019, when the cab signal technology was changed to allow any Positive Train Control (PTC)-equipped locomotive to lead a train on the line. Union Pacific has also repainted most locomotives that came from previous companies such as the Chicago and Northwestern Railway and the Cotton Belt (St. Louis and Southwestern Railway). The implementation of PTC on most rail lines in Chicago has recently prevented many older locomotives without the technology to lead trains, forcing photographers to look harder for the most historical trains.

However, change was not always a bad thing in the eyes of the railfan. In late 2020, the Canadian National painted five "heritage unit" locomotives into the schemes of their predecessor railroads such as Wisconsin Central Ltd. and the Elgin Joliet and Eastern Railway. As Canadian Pacific rebuilt older EMDs into SD70ACus, ten of them were painted into CP's older maroon and grey paint scheme as well as five engines painted to commemorate branches of the Canadian Military. Metra has purchased new locomotives including former-Amtrak EMD F59PHIs, one of which was specially painted into the Chicago and Northwestern paint scheme. The ever-changing scene in railroads certainly keeps the photographer entertained in some way or another.

Not only does the Midwest have some of the most interesting trains in themselves, it has some of the best photographic locations at which one can incorporate something interesting in a photo of a train. With Chicagoland's vast network of extinct railroad companies, many of these fallen rail companies live on in vintage signals, heritage locomotives, passenger depots, and bridges around the area. Popular locations include: The Tower B-12 signal bridge in Franklin Park, IL, CP Morgan in downtown Chicago with hundreds of passenger trains a day, and the Rochelle, IL, Railroad Park where Burlington Northern Santa Fe and Union Pacific mainlines cross. All of these locations are incredibly timeless and well-documented in Chicagoland railfanning, but perhaps the most famous spot for all of Chicago railroading is Rondout Tower near Libertyville,

Illinois. Rondout sits about 32 miles north of Chicago on the Canadian Pacific mainline to Milwaukee, Wisconsin and is the junction at which the Metra Fox Lake Subdivision begins and the former-Elgin Joliet and Eastern crosses. The plant is complete with sixteen vintage searchlight signals, as well as an interlocking tower dating back to the days of Milwaukee Road steam.

While these locations are extremely popular, there are some which simply do not get their fair share of documentation. From small Wisconsin towns to big cities with hidden shots, many stories in the Midwest are awaiting their turn to be told. The first of many is Tiffany, Wisconsin, on the Union Pacific main to Janesville, with its 150-year-old limestone arch bridge spanning Turtle Creek. The Union Pacific Harvard Subdivision's plethora of vintage searchlight signals lining the former CNW mainline for miles is also under-appreciated, as well as UP's infamous street running in Rockford, IL, which has little documentation.

About 50 miles northwest of Chicago is the Illinois Railway Museum, the largest train museum in the country. Hundreds of unique, vintage railcars and locomotives call this museum home. Run exclusively by volunteers, the museum is primarily open in the summer months when steam, electric, and diesel trains are all run for passenger ridership or demonstration purposes. With no shortage of photo opportunities and a large preservation of railroading history from around the country, the IRM is a very important location to many railfans from Chicago and around the country.

There is far too little previous representation of many of Chicagoland's most unique locations of railroading, and this collection puts a spotlight on many unseen locations in the greater Chicagoland area. It is important to showcase the most common trains in some of the most frequented locations, but it is also crucial that the less-known areas of the region are under the spotlight. Our philosophy as photographers and railfans has always been to prioritize documenting what is going to become history the soonest, such as older locomotives set to be replaced by new ones. We also emphasize finding trains that differ from the usual mainline locomotives in locations that truly stand out. Adding a historical building or remnant of a previous railroad always spices up a photograph, and we find it important to focus on not just the train but what surrounds the train in many cases. It takes hard work to track down and follow these trains, but the era of social media has benefitted railfans making it easier to communicate information. It is also important to photograph every train that passes by no matter where one may find themselves and not only focus on the more "interesting" types of locomotives or train movements. One day many years ahead, a picture of a specific train in a specific location may simply be a thing of the past.

Chicagoland's North and Western suburbs are a true testament to days gone by meeting the future of railroading. Anything and everything can be found in the north and west region of Chicagoland, an area that truly gets far less credit than it deserves. To the railfans who have grown up in the region or have moved to Chicagoland, the city, the suburbs, and the trains will always be one thing to them. It will forever be home.

With an empty hopper train in tow, Union Pacific 1038, an EMD GP60, leads a southbound local to Troy Grove, Illinois. The 1038 is passing the famous Dekalb coaling tower in this photo, with reflections shown from a prior rainstorm. [*James Keats Jr.*]

1

UNION PACIFIC GENEVA SUBDIVISION

The Union Pacific Geneva Subdivision is easily the most popular and busy trackage in all of the Northwest suburbs. Owned previously by the Chicago and Northwestern Railroad until 1995, it is now UP's lifeline to their main country-wide system, running straight from Chicago, Illinois, and into Iowa, Nebraska, and all the way to the West Coast. The Geneva connects with the famous transcontinental railroad, making it one of the busiest lines for double stack, manifest, unit, and any other train traversing the United States. In terms of Metra, the Geneva Subdivision is called the Union Pacific West Line. Starting in Chicago, Metra runs via the Union Pacific through populous towns such as Elmhurst, Glen Ellyn, Wheaton, Geneva, and many more. The namesake of the line is Geneva, IL, itself, as Geneva was once the end of the line for Chicago and Northwestern passenger service. But now as it is extended to Elburn, IL, Metra travels nearly 45 miles to the fields of the western suburbs.

The Geneva is extremely busy on any day of the week, as Metra service is non-stop between Chicago and Elburn, as well as the Union Pacific trains going cross-country. With such heavy traffic, there must be a yard for the UP to work in and out of, and indeed there is. Union Pacific's Proviso Yard, located just outside of Elmhurst, IL, is one of the largest rail yards in the entire country. With connecting tracks to not only the Union Pacific Geneva Subdivision, Proviso Yard connects to that of the Indiana Harbor Belt, a transfer railroad connecting all of Chicagoland. Working out of Proviso to the east, many important junctions sit near the city of Chicago. One of which being Tower A-2, a large interlocking where the Geneva Subdivision crosses three Metra mainlines all at once. A-2 is also home to one of the last manned interlocking towers. Numerous CNW-era artifacts sit near the city, including vintage CNW searchlights and E-Type signals seen in this chapter.

Working west of Elmhurst, there are many popular railfanning locations. First there is Elmhurst, a Metra station sitting at the mouth of Proviso Yard. Then, there is Glen Ellyn, with a soon-to-be-replaced CNW depot, and then follows West Chicago, where the Geneva Subdivision crosses the former-Elgin Joliet and Eastern at JB Tower. After West Chicago, Metra starts to work its way into "the sticks," as the towns get smaller and the depots fewer and farther in between. Metra ends its service at Elburn, but the freight traffic does not stop there. Once the Union Pacific opens up past Metra territory, the line runs straight west past towns such as Cortland, Dekalb, Rochelle, and Nelson. First of those being Cortland, with its now-removed CNW searchlight signals. Next is Dekalb, another popular location in Chicagoland, with its steam-era coaling tower and branch line off the main to Troy Grove, IL. Moving west to Rochelle sits one of Chicagoland's most recognizable locations. The Rochelle Railroad Park is easily one of the most visited locations in the area, with the Geneva Subdivision crossing the equally popular Burlington Northern Santa Fe main. Finally, even further than Rochelle, sits Nelson, IL. Nelson is the sight of not only another coaling tower, but three signal bridges containing, in all, over twenty CNW searchlights. The Geneva Subdivision is one of, if not the busiest, subdivisions in the entire state of Illinois, with, on some days, over seventy-five Metra and Union Pacific trains traversing the tracks. The Geneva shows Chicagoland railroading at its finest, a hustling and bustling triple and double-track main providing some of the best action around.

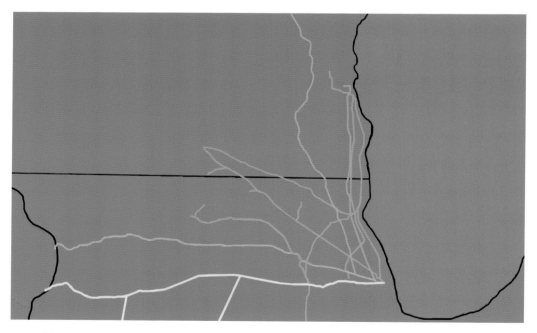

This map of the Union Pacific Geneva Subdivision and its branch lines at Dekalb and Nelson, Illinois, show the former Chicago and Northwestern working its way west into Iowa from Chicago.

To most, Chicago is known more for its snowy winters than its trains. After running through the snow with a Metra commuter train, Metra 147 (EMD F40PH) sits in Ogilvie Transportation Center next to Union Pacific Yard 711, an EMD GP15AC. [*David Zeman*]

Ogilvie Transportation Center is the beginning of the Metra trains that run on all three Union Pacific lines. Metra 90, the Chicago & Northwestern heritage unit, awaits an evening departure from OTC, with a Metra EMD F40PH and another Metra train arriving in the background. [*David Zeman*]

An inbound Metra train from one of the Union Pacific lines shoves into Ogilvie Transportation Center with an EMD F40PH for power. OTC itself is barely visible on the right side of the image. [*David Zeman*]

Metra 132, an EMD F40PH, leads an outbound Union Pacific West Line commuter train under the searchlight signals at Tower A-2 in Chicago, Illinois, on a cloudy winter day. [*David Zeman*]

East of Proviso Yard is the only section of the Geneva Subdivision on which a locomotive from another railroad can lead due to signal restrictions. Case in point, here is CSXT 8350, an EMD SD40-2, leading a westbound coke pellet train under the unique Chicago & Northwestern Signals in Oak Park, Illinois, in the spring of 2020. [*David Zeman*]

In River Forest, Illinois, the Geneva Subdivision ducks under the CN Waukesha Subdivision. This portion of the Waukesha Subdivision hardly ever sees trains nowadays; however, the Geneva Subdivision provides plenty of action with countless Metra and freight trains per day. Here is Metra 168, an EMD F40PH, ascending from the dip under the CN in River Forest with an outbound commuter train. [*David Zeman*]

Just like many major railroad yards, Union Pacific's Proviso Yard sports a fair amount of sidelined power. Seen here is a chunk of that power, including a mix of both standard cabs and wide cabs. An industry downturn due to the COVID-19 pandemic has resulted in these lines growing far bigger than seen in this January 2019 view. [*David Dupuis*]

Back in 2019, Union Pacific Big Boy locomotive 4014 rolled through the Chicagoland area with an excursion special traversing a large portion of the country. Here the train is seen rolling past the Chicago and Northwestern depot in Glen Ellyn, Illinois, heading for West Chicago. This shot also captures the extreme mass of people that turned out to catch a glimpse of the classic giant. [*James Keats Jr.*]

Union Pacific operates some of the most impressively painted locomotives out of any railroad. One of the most extravagant is the UP 1943, an EMD SD70AH, which honors members of the military. Here 1943 is seen leading a westbound business train past the College Avenue Metra Station in Wheaton, Illinois. [*David Zeman*]

An unusually colorful consist led by Union Pacific 2002, an EMD SD70M painted for the Salt Lake Olympics, heads east under the former-Chicago Aurora & Elgin bridge in Wheaton, Illinois. [*David Zeman*]

An eastbound Union Pacific stack train led by a UP GE AC45CCTE ducks under the intermediate signals west of the interlocking at University in Wheaton, Illinois. [*David Zeman*]

Two sister Union Pacific General Electric locomotives lead a cross-country container train east by the famous JB Tower in West Chicago, Illinois. This junction marks where the former Chicago and Northwestern and Elgin Joliet and Eastern railroads crossed each other. These extinct railroads are now owned by the giant class ones of UP and CN. [*James Keats Jr.*]

Metra 84, one of the newest EMD F59PHI units on the Metra roster, shoves an inbound train past JB Tower to downtown Chicago. With these afternoon Metra runs, West Chicago turns into a railfanning hotspot, as the diamonds at JB provide a great setting for back-to-back trains on both the Union Pacific and Canadian National. [*James Keats Jr.*]

The Geneva Subdivision was formerly owned by the Chicago & Northwestern Railroad, therefore seeing the CNW heritage unit on this line is quite appropriate. In this photo from the spring of 2018, UP 1995, the CNW-painted EMD SD70ACe, leads an eastbound manifest train over the Fox River in Geneva, Illinois. On the bridge itself, a faded CNW logo sign can still be seen. [*David Zeman*]

Union Pacific 6706, the last Chicago and Northwestern painted GE AC4400CW on the roster, leads an eastbound double-stack container train to UP's Global II intermodal facility through the small town of Elburn, Illinois. The 6706 is a reminder to railfans of UP's CNW heritage, especially after the popular "twin" original paint units of 8646 and 8701 were repainted. [*James Keats Jr.*]

The Chicago & Northwestern was absorbed by the Union Pacific in 1995, but some of the locomotives from the CNW lasted well over twenty years later. Unfortunately, these locomotives only lasted in CNW paint until early 2018. As seen in 2017, CNW 8646 and CNW 8701, both GE C44-9Ws, lead an eastbound intermodal/autorack transfer through Meredith, Illinois. [*David Zeman*]

Union Pacific 1111, the "Powered by our People" special paint EMD SD70ACe, leads a westbound business train to Nelson, Iowa, between the Chicago and Northwestern searchlight signals at Cortland, Illinois. These vintage searchlights have since been replaced by newer LED signals, bringing an end to one of the most popular Chicagoland railfanning locations. [*James Keats Jr.*]

UPY 709, a classic EMD GP15 locomotive, leads a sister GP15 with a local freight to Troy Grove, Illinois. The local is seen here diverting off the Geneva Subdivision at Dekalb, Illinois, and past the very popular Chicago and North Western coaling tower. This tower has sat over the Geneva Subdivision for 100+ years, serving as a constant reminder to the CNW's steam filled past. [*James Keats Jr.*]

UPY GP15 709 again with its local freight, as it works its way through the very small town of Elva, Illinois. Elva sits just south of Dekalb on Union Pacific's Troy Grove Branch/Subdivision. Also included in this shot is the large, vintage grain silos along the tracks. With the subdivision rolling through farm country, it is common to see grain silos and elevators lining the tracks. [*James Keats Jr.*]

Union Pacific 8568, an EMD SD70ACe, rolls west past the Rochelle Railroad Park, and approaches the BNSF diamonds about 20 feet behind this picture. On a good day in Rochelle, a railfan could see up to fifty trains on the two giant Class I Railroads. [*James Keats Jr.*]

Union Pacific 1989, an EMD SD70ACe, works its way through Rochelle, Illinois, sporting its Rio Grande heritage livery. The 1989 is leading one of UP's most important cross-country trains here, on a double stack high priority run to Los Angeles. Also featured is the extremely popular Rochelle Railroad Park. An instant hit with any visitors, the park is situated directly in between the UP Geneva Subdivision, and the BNSF Aurora Subdivision. [*James Keats Jr.*]

Union Pacific 8817, an EMD SD70AH, leads a westbound continuous ballast-conveyor train out of Rochelle, Illinois. This train carries railroad ballast for the rail bed, and a conveyor system brings the rock to the rear of the train for discharging into the rails. Also shown in the background is UP's large Global 3 facility for loading double-stack container trains. [*James Keats Jr.*]

It is usually difficult to get a photo of three different generations of GE locomotives meeting; however, such a meet was seen in the fall of 2018. From left to right, UP 5727 (GE AC44CWCTE) and UP 7962 (GE AC45CCTE) are passed by UP 2639 (ET44AH) in Nelson, Illinois. [*David Zeman*]

Nelson, Illinois, is known amongst Chicago-area railfans as a scene that is stuck in time. Trademarked by a coaling tower and an abundance of searchlight signals, the scene offered at Nelson is not an easy one to come by anywhere else. In this January 2019 photograph, a westbound intermodal train transitions through the scene with a mix of GE and EMD wide cab power up front. [*David Dupuis*]

2

CANADIAN PACIFIC CHICAGO/ ELGIN SUBDIVISIONS

The Canadian Pacific Elgin Subdivision is one of CP's mainlines to the west and the hub of Illinois operations. The Elgin Subdivision has the diversity any rail fan would want in the area. From small-town Metra service to bustling yards, the Elgin contains some of the most popular railfanning locations and busiest junctions in the Chicagoland area. The Elgin Subdivision starts just outside of Chicago at Tower A-5, running through some of Chicago's most populous western suburbs such as Franklin Park, Wood Dale, Itasca, Elgin, and many more. Metra service is extremely prevalent on this subdivision, as one could spend an entire day watching Metra trains running from sunrise to sunset and beyond. As mentioned, the Elgin Subdivision holds some of the most popular railfanning locations in the entire state, the most popular of which being Tower B-12. B-12 is, as indicated by the number, 12 miles from Union Station in Chicago. The tower itself has been moved several blocks west of the actual interlocking, but a large signal bridge still remains, guarding the large junction between the Canadian Pacific, Canadian National, and the Indiana Harbor Belt.

With the plethora of freight and passenger movements through this popular railfanning destination, many railfans find their way to B-12 for their favorite trains. Just west of Tower B-12 sits Canadian Pacific's massive Bensenville Yard, the hub of Midwestern operations outside their equally large yard in St. Paul, Minnesota. Anything and everything on CP rolling through Chicago is most likely destined or coming from Bensenville. With not only CP using this yard, railroads such as the UP and IHB run transfer trains to and from Bensenville to bridge the gaps between other yards in the area.

Bensenville Yard does not define the Elgin Subdivision all by itself though, as outside the hustle and bustle of Bensenville sit many other important junctions and destinations for the railroad. The Elgin Subdivision crosses the Canadian National main to Joliet out near Bartlett, as well as the Union Pacific Belvidere Subdivision just outside of Elgin. West of the inbound and outbound frenzy of Metra commuter trains is the small, single track CP main to Savanna, Illinois. This portion of the Elgin Subdivision, which is in fact beyond Elgin, is more commonly referred to as the Chicago Subdivision. The Chicago Subdivision travels through small towns such as Hampshire and Genoa, Illinois, and a few larger towns such as Byron and Pingree Grove. While at first appearing bland, the trackage west of Elgin is filled with artifacts of days gone by, including vintage pole lines lining the tracks and various signage from the days of the Milwaukee Road. The Elgin and Chicago Subdivisions host some of the most recognizable railfanning locations in Chicagoland, earning their place for representation.

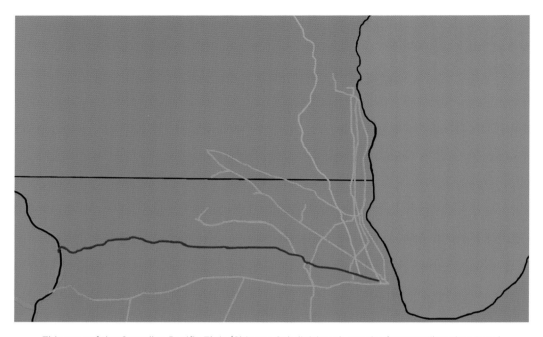

This map of the Canadian Pacific Elgin/Chicago Subdivision shows the former Milwaukee Road working its way west into Iowa from Chicago.

Opposite page

Above: With a plume of black smoke, Metra F40PH-3 107 charges west out of Elmwood Park with an Elgin bound commuter train. [*James Keats Jr.*]

Below: One of ten EMD SD70ACus painted in Canadian Pacific's grey and maroon scheme leads a freight train bound for the C&M Subdivision east through River Grove, Illinois. [*David Zeman*]

Canadian Pacific moves cars to and from their Schiller Container Park Yard by running transfers between Schiller Park and Bensenville Yard. One of those transfers is seen here under the signals at Tower B-12 in Franklin Park, Illinois, powered by CP 5108, an EMD SD40-3. [*David Zeman*]

A freshly rebuilt and repainted Canadian Pacific EMD SD70ACu leads an eastbound mixed freight train through Tower B-12 in Franklin Park, Illinois. [*David Zeman*]

A Metra F59PHI rolls west from Chicago with an outbound train under the famous Tower B-12 signal bridge in Franklin Park. The Tower B-12 signal bridge is easily one of the most popular locations in the area, seeing a highly diverse selection of trains. [*James Keats Jr.*]

Canadian Pacific's business train, powered by CP 1401 (GMD FP9A), a GMD F9B, and two more FP9As, heads westbound through Franklin Park, Illinois, at Tower B-12 before going into Bensenville Yard for the night. [*David Zeman*]

Another outbound Metra with F40PH-3 107 again rolls through Franklin Park, this time passing the actual restored and relocated Tower B-12. This is the original tower from the CP/CN diamonds, about a half-mile east from where the tower now sits. [*James Keats Jr.*]

Indiana Harbor Belt 4015, an EMD GP40-2, and an IHB "Genset" locomotive rebuild by NRE Rail lead an autorack transfer train into Canadian Pacific's Bensenville Yard. Several times a week, the IHB runs its own trains into Bensenville Yard with their eye-catching orange and black paint. Unfortunately, due to roster modernization, both units in this shot are off IHBs roster today. [*James Keats Jr.*]

The east end of Canadian Pacific's Bensenville Yard is busy 365 days of the year. This day was no different, as an eastbound CP oil train for the Belt Railway of Chicago with CP GE AC44CW 8522 leading meets an Intermodal pulldown job with CP 3053, an EMD GP38-2. [*James Keats Jr.*]

In late 2019, Canadian Pacific unveiled their heritage fleet of locomotives in their classic gray and maroon paint scheme. The first two examples, 7010 and 7015, sit on display for a company photo shoot inside Bensenville yard. [*James Keats Jr.*]

Metra 405, the Milwaukee Road-painted MPI MP36PH, leads an outbound Milwaukee District West train past Tower B-17 in Bensenville, Illinois. On the right side, the Chicago skyline can be seen in the distance as well as a Canadian Pacific EMD locomotive in Bensenville Yard. [*David Zeman*]

Metra F59PHI No. 85 shoves an inbound train past the Bartlett, Illinois depot. This station was beautifully restored and is now a trackside museum for the city of Bartlett. The new Metra Bartlett station now sits directly behind this depot. [*James Keats Jr.*]

Once in a great while, the railroad will do something next to impossible. This train was incredibly odd and unusual, as it is a Canadian Pacific weed sprayer train being powered by a Ferromex EMD GP38-2. These trains typically have Canadian Pacific locomotives for power, and Ferromex GP38-2s are incredibly rare to see north of the Mexican border except for places like Texas. [*David Zeman*]

The modern Metra Rail roster is extremely diverse and unique. Here a doubleheader works its way through Elgin with an EMD F59PHI No. 84 and a MPI MP36PH No. 426. Also shown is an old Pullman coach behind the power rebuilt from a Chicago and Northwestern coach. [*James Keats Jr.*]

CP 5966, an EMD SD40-2, splits the Hampshire ID sign and some classic codeline rolling into Hampshire, Illinois, with the weed sprayer train. When shooting this train, railfans have to be very careful to get out of the way before they get sprayed with weed killer! [*James Keats Jr.*]

Opposite page

Above: Metra 81, an EMD F59PHI, reaches the end of the line at Big Timber Road in Elgin, Illinois, with its outbound train from Chicago. After dropping passengers at the station, the train would then wait to head back into the city on an inbound run. [*David Zeman*]

Below: Canadian Pacific 5966, a vintage EMD SD40-2, is in charge of this "Weed-Sprayer" train making its way east through the swamps of Starks, Illinois. This train is very unique, as once every year CP runs it up and down their Subdivisions to kill trackside weeds. [*James Keats Jr.*]

3

UNION PACIFIC
BELVIDERE SUBDIVISION

Union Pacific's Belvidere Subdivision is not exactly the busiest line in the world. Seeing a maximum of five or so trains per day, the Belvidere Subdivision services a handful of local industries, including the Chrysler Corporation Belvidere assembly plant. Starting from Union Pacific's West Chicago Yard, the Belvidere Subdivision works its way through small towns such as Huntley and Marengo, and large towns such as Elgin and Rockford.

As well as these towns, the Belvidere Subdivision is the lifeline to the United States' largest rail museum. The Illinois Railway Museum sits just feet from the Belvidere Subdivision, and with an interchange track just outside of downtown Union, anything in the IRM has most likely traveled on the UP.

While the Subdivision doesn't see the amount of trains its fellow Union Pacific lines in the area do, it has one very important thing going for it: heritage. The subdivision sits on former Galena and Chicago Union Railroad trackage. Built in the 1800s, most of the G&CU right-of-way has remained the same. Chicago and Northwestern owned the line until 1995 when Union Pacific took over.

The best hidden gem of all is Union Pacific's trackage west of Belvidere and into Rockford, Illinois. This former Chicago and Northwestern trackage winds into Illinois' third biggest city and crosses the Rock River in downtown. The real prize comes just before downtown Rockford on a small branch line known simply to the locals as the "KD." This branch off the mainline was once the CNW Kenosha Division, an east-by-west connecting route from Rockford to Kenosha, Wisconsin. Now the majority is ripped up, and the small branch only traverses about seven miles to Loves Park, IL. On the way to Loves Park, the Union Pacific encounters one of its most unique portions of trackage in the entire country, as for almost a full mile it runs straight down the middle of a street. Modern-day street running is hard to come by, and on a Class I it is nearly non-existent. As local railfans know, the Belvidere, while slow, has some great shots and great heritage to photograph.

This map of the Union Pacific Belvidere Subdivision, and its branch line at Rockford, Illinois, shows the former Chicago and Northwestern working its way west into northern Illinois from West Chicago.

One of Union Pacific's mainline autorack trains, led by Union Pacific GE ES44AC No. 8173, rolls through the small town of Huntley, IL. Huntley is the pure definition of an old railroad town. Built around the Chicago and Northwestern originally, it has rapidly expanded into a large suburb. [*James Keats Jr.*]

On this early morning loaded eastbound auto train, Union Pacific 1038, a four-axle EMD GP60 locomotive, takes charge all by its lonesome. It is very rare to see four-axle yard power beyond UP's yards on large mainline trains, but with a power shortage in late 2019, this shot was possible. [*James Keats Jr.*]

Union Pacific 7334, an interesting rebuilt AC6000CW, takes a westbound auto train by "Signal 352," a vintage searchlight signal along the IRM main. Many people see the two side-by-side mains and wonder how close they actually are to each other. This shot stands testament to that. [*James Keats Jr.*]

With the Illinois Railway Museum right beside the mainline, a rare weekend Belvidere train is a treat to museumgoers. Shown here is UP 4033, an EMD SD70M, leading a westbound auto train by the museum. The smoke in the sky behind 4033 is that of SLSF (Frisco) 1630, IRM's famed 2-10-0 decapod. [*James Keats Jr.*]

The Union Pacific often does not let locomotives from other railroads lead on their mainlines due to UP's unique signal system. The Belvidere Subdivision is primarily track warrant control, meaning no locomotives with specific signals are needed. This made this late summer evening run possible, as two CSX GEs lead a westbound train to Belvidere. [*James Keats Jr.*]

On the Loves Park branch, UPY 608, an EMD GP15 encounters the famous street running portion of the main. This section of the former Chicago and Northwestern "KD" line dates back to the early steam days, also being one of the last street running sections in the state of Illinois. Here is the local making its way south in golden light back to Rockford. [*James Keats Jr.*]

Opposite page

Above: Taking it west of Belvidere, here is Union Pacific's Rockford and Loves Park local making its way over the Rock River in Rockford, IL. This local is being led by a classic GP15, originally built for the Missouri Pacific. Looking closer, this train is running in a rather odd configuration due to the UP having to drop their last car before heading north to the Loves Park branch for work. [*James Keats Jr.*]

Below: A three-unit Union Pacific local, led by the UP 5245, a former Rio Grande EMD GP40-2, leads southbound to Belvidere past "The Symbol" sculpture in Rockford. With UP's roster constantly changing, many locomotives are moved around and renumbered, but not the 5245, as it is the last GP in the 5000-number series and has been based out of Belvidere since 2013. [*James Keats Jr.*]

4

UNION PACIFIC HARVARD SUBDIVISION

The Union Pacific Harvard Subdivision easily holds the title as the most underrated subdivision in all of Chicagoland. Known as the "Muscle Line" to some local railfans, the Harvard Subdivision runs from downtown Chicago's Ogilvie Transportation Center to Janesville, Wisconsin. Owned by Union Pacific since 1995, the Harvard Subdivision holds some of the best-kept secrets in the Midwest. Referred to as the Union Pacific Northwest Line on Metra's timetables, it runs straight northwest to Harvard, Illinois. The subdivision traverses through some of Chicagoland's most popular suburbs such as Arlington Heights, Des Plaines, Barrington, Palatine, and Crystal Lake. Most Metra traffic stops at Crystal Lake and returns eastbound to Chicago, but a handful of trains make the long trip to Harvard, IL. Harvard is just south of the Wisconsin border, and is the furthest Metra runs from the city of Chicago, at a staggering 63 miles. Some of the most popular locations on the Metra portion of the Harvard are at junctions with other railroads. First off is Clybourn, which is just outside of downtown Chicago. The Kenosha Subdivision splits from the Harvard at Clybourn and heads north while the Harvard Subdivision goes northwesterly. The Harvard also crosses through a junction known as Deval in Des Plaines, IL. Deval is the crossing point of three railroad lines all at once, with the Union Pacific Harvard and Milwaukee Subdivisions and the Canadian National Waukesha Subdivision all coming together. Moving west, the Harvard crosses the former Elgin Joliet and Eastern (now CN) at Barrington. From there the traffic slows, and the main cuts down from a triple-track to a double-track, as Metra works its way west into towns such as Fox River Grove and Cary. Once Metra reaches Crystal Lake Jct., things get much more interesting. A bustling CNW yard and diamond in years gone by, Crystal Lake Jct. now features a very unique manned junction house for the UP McHenry Branch. The McHenry Branch sees limited traffic, with only five Metra trains per day and an occasional UP local. The branch sits on former CNW Lake Geneva Subdivision territory, as the line was once a popular passenger route to Lake Geneva, Wisconsin. McHenry, IL, is the last stop nowadays with its 1912 depot standing guard next to the tracks. As Metra works its way into Harvard and the passenger service stops, the real fun begins. A largely undocumented portion of the Harvard Subdivision is its Union Pacific freight traffic. Most trains come from Proviso, hop on the Harvard Subdivision mainline at Seeger in Des Plaines, and then make their way north to Janesville. The Harvard Subdivision is not what it used to be, as the main traffic source, the Janesville General Motors plant, was closed years ago. Now the Harvard is simply a local freight and grain lifeline, serving various grain elevators and small industries along the way.

While the traffic has slowed, some of the interesting power has stayed the same. Up until late 2019, Union Pacific powered a majority of their trains with their EMD SD40N rebuilds. Unfortunately, when their cab signal system was no longer needed to travel on the line and the Harvard Subdivision had its signal technology upgraded, these locomotives vanished from Harvard trains. While the muscle of modern EMD SD40Ns disappeared, the mostly undocumented locations north of Metra territory have not—yet. Every signal block on the Harvard Subdivision north of Harvard is protected by searchlight-type signals. The Harvard is one of those lines that was just caught in the past and never updated, leaving CNW history littering the single-track subdivision. While many find their way to photograph the searchlight signals, there is a single location that defines the Harvard Subdivision. This location sits in the small town of Tiffany, Wisconsin, just south of Janesville.

Tiffany easily holds the best-kept secret of the entire Midwest: the Tiffany Parkway Stone Arch bridge. As of 2020, the classic limestone arch bridge is 150 years old. Built by the CNW in the days of steam, the arch bridge still stands and serves the Harvard Subdivision trains every day. The bridge stands testament to all railfans that the Harvard subdivision is worth photographing, and worth documentation. With the colorful history of the entire Harvard Subdivision, it is impossible to talk about the northern suburbs without mentioning it, as it is one of the most historical and important subdivisions in the area.

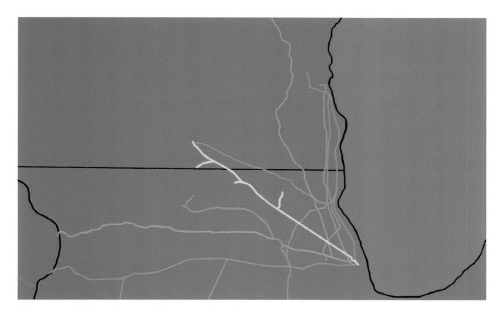

This map of the Union Pacific Harvard Subdivision, and its branch lines at Crystal Lake, IL, Harvard, IL, and Clinton, WI, show the former Chicago and Northwestern working its way west to Janesville from Chicago.

Mere miles from Ogilvie Transportation Center (and the official start of the Harvard Subdivision) lies the former Chicago and North Western Railway's "Low Line." Once providing rail service to many downtown Chicago-based customers, this line once extended all the way out to what is today Navy Pier. Today, however, the line is abandoned east of the infamous "always up" Kinzie Street Railroad Bridge, and the only customer remaining is the *Chicago Tribune*. A few days a week, a Union Pacific local train comes down to spot the Tribune, and such is seen here as UP 1430, an EMD GP40-2, pulls a couple box cars out from the industry. [*David Dupuis*]

At Clybourn, the Union Pacific Harvard Subdivision continues in a north-west direction as the Kenosha Subdivision splits to go north along Lake Michigan. The Kenosha Subdivision tracks can be seen on the left in this photo, as an outbound Metra train on the Harvard Subdivision led by EMD F40 No. 144 comes under the signal bridge at Clybourn. [*David Zeman*]

Military trains rarely make it down the Harvard Subdivision. In March of 2020, UP 7477 (GE AC45CCTE) holds in Mount Prospect, IL, with an eastbound train of military vehicles. [*David Zeman*]

On the Harvard Subdivision, unit grain trains and mixed freight trains usually run separately to their destinations. This rare mixed freight-grain train combination is on the journey to Janesville as it passes through Arlington Heights, IL, on a very cold winter day with UP 2007 (EMD SD40N) leading Union Pacific GE engines, plus a Norfolk Southern locomotive in the mix. [*David Zeman*]

METX 166, an EMD F40PH, powers an outbound express passenger train past the Arlington Heights, Illinois, train station. [*David Zeman*]

UP 1972, an EMD SD40N, pilots a westbound empty grain train past the passenger depot in Arlington Heights, IL. [*David Zeman*]

Until mid-2019, Union Pacific ran a tri-weekly train from Proviso Yard to Janesville and back. Photographed on 10/8/2018, UP 1972 (EMD SD40N) leads the westbound run through Arlington Heights, IL. [*David Zeman*]

There are several relics of the Chicago and Northwestern still present on the Harvard Subdivision, some of which being original CNW signal bridges with modern signals. METX 90, the CNW-painted F59PHI, ducks under one of these old signal bridges at Arlington Park, Illinois. [*David Zeman*]

Many of the stops on the Harvard Subdivision feature impressive passenger stations. One of the most impressive stations on the line is in Palatine, Illinois, seen here being passed by a westbound empty grain train with Union Pacific 2007 (EMD SD40N) leading. [*David Zeman*]

In this rare and unique move, Metra 90: The CNW heritage EMD F59PHI, and Metra 402, The State of Illinois' commemorative MPI MP36PH, take an employee special over the Fox River. This was the first time a MP36 locomotive ventured onto the Harvard Subdivision, as bridge restrictions downtown limit where these heavy locomotives can run. [*James Keats Jr.*]

Crystal Lake, Illinois, a once large junction, now just houses a few rip tracks and this small house. This is one of the last manned switch houses in the United States on a major railroad. The "switchtenders shanty" is shown here with a Janesville bound local with UP 1843, an EMD SD40N, leading. [*James Keats Jr.*]

With Metra's acquisition of many former Amtrak EMD F59PHIs, they sent a few to the Union Pacific Subdivisions. Here is Metra 75, making its maiden voyage on the Harvard Subdivision. [*James Keats Jr.*]

A repainted Metra EMD F40PH-3 No. 178, sits next to the over 100-year-old CNW depot in McHenry, Illinois. On a once-prominent line that saw daily service to Lake Geneva, Wisconsin, this is the furthest passenger service goes nowadays. [*James Keats Jr.*]

Another interesting location on the Harvard Subdivision is Ridgefield, IL. This true railroad town has only a few houses and a church, along with this Chicago and Northwestern town sign and the daily Metra trains. Here Metra EMD F40PH-3 144 does track speed past this CNW sign. [*James Keats Jr.*]

An inbound Metra led by a Nippon-Sharyo cab car rolls out of Woodstock headed for Chicago. This shot showcases the first snow of winter 2020, with snow covered trees still showing hints of fall. [*James Keats Jr.*]

Union Pacific 1430 leads a short local past the 1920s built Woodstock, Illinois, station. This depot, while built over 100 years ago, gets constant refurbishments by the historical centered town of Woodstock, made popular from blockbuster movies. [*James Keats Jr.*]

Showing two generations of Metra paint schemes, Metra 121 rolls through Harvard, passing a train set resting for the weekend. Both of these trains are led by EMD F40PH-3s, with the newer of the two being the more colorful paint scheme Metra 177. [*James Keats Jr.*]

Metra F59PHI 90, along with sister F59PHI 75, shove an inbound train off the old CNW Kenosha Division and past the old CNW freight house in the background of Harvard, Illinois. Harvard is the farthest Metra that goes from Chicago on its entire system, at a whopping 63 miles. [*James Keats Jr.*]

Union Pacific 1972, a EMD SD40N leads a southbound local from Janesville, Wisconsin, splitting the searchlights at Lawrence, IL. With constant improvements made to the Harvard Subdivision, these signals will be the first to come down in mid-2021. [*James Keats Jr.*]

Union Pacific 1914, a UP rebuild EMD SD40N, splits a set of searchlight signals deep in the forests of Wisconsin. This was one of the last locals on the Harvard Subdivision with UP's SD40N, as other locals were expanded and used four-axle power. [*James Keats Jr.*]

UP 1843, an EMD SD40N heading for Janesville, Wisconsin, splitting rather off-center searchlights in Sharon, WI. These signals are one of the more popular sets of lights on the Harvard Subdivision, as many crews claim they think one day they'll hit them as they go by. [*James Keats Jr.*]

The eastbound Union Pacific local from Janesville to Chicago runs away from the setting sun with a GP40-2 leading two more UP locomotives as it splits the searchlight signals in Sharon, WI. [*David Zeman*]

Many of Union Pacific's fallen flag engines have been repainted over the years, and rarely do the engines that remain in fallen flag paint come to the Harvard Subdivision. UP 1158, a former-Cotton Belt EMD GP60, is in charge of a sixty-car freight train to Janesville under the cover of darkness at Clinton, WI. [*David Zeman*]

Union Pacific 1145, an EMD GP60, leads a southbound local down the Stateline Branch of the Harvard Subdivision. The 1145 splits some trees as it approaches the state line back into Illinois and South Beloit. [*James Keats Jr.*]

Easily one of the best-kept secret gems of the Midwest has to be the Tiffany, Wisconsin, stone arch bridge. Built over 150 years ago for Chicago and Northwestern, here we see Union Pacific 1914, a EMD SD40N rebuild of CNW heritage itself, leading a train over the limestone arch bridge. [*James Keats Jr.*]

After the famous SD40N pilots disappeared, anything was possible on the Harvard Subdivision. Here is Union Pacific 4703, an EMD SD70M, coming into Janesville, Wisconsin, with an empty grain train for Evansville, Wisconsin. [*James Keats Jr.*]

5

CANADIAN NATIONAL LEITHTON SUBDIVISION

The Canadian National Leithton Subdivision reinvented the way CN took trains through Chicagoland. Since the acquisition of the trackage from the Elgin Joliet & Eastern in 2009, CN has used this line to take their trains around Chicago rather than through the congested inner-city trackage. As a main run-through for northbound and southbound freight trains between Wisconsin and locations south and east of Chicago, the twenty-thirty trains a day travel painlessly through suburbs in Chicagoland. Even though the former "J" ran all the way from North Chicago, Illinois, to Gary, Indiana, the focus on the Leithton Subdivision for this book extends only as far south as West Chicago, IL, at JB Tower.

JB Tower is the railroad's junction with the Union Pacific Geneva Subdivision, and the original EJ&E tower still remains here. Following the trackage north takes freight trains through Chicago suburbs such as Elgin, Hoffman Estates, Lake Zurich, and Mundelein. The "J" crosses the Canadian Pacific Elgin Subdivision in Elgin, IL, at Spaulding, and further north crosses the Union Pacific Harvard Subdivision at Barrington, IL. At Leithton, the junction with the Waukesha Subdivision in Mundelein, IL, traffic on the "J" turns onto the Waukesha to head north towards Fond du Lac, Wisconsin. A southbound on the Waukesha Subdivision typically turns right at Leithton to go west and south on the "J" rather than continuing south towards Schiller Park. The Leithton Subdivision continues east of Mundelein, crossing the Canadian Pacific at Rondout Tower and the Union Pacific at Upton in North Chicago where the line ends a few miles beyond the crossing. Most of the train traffic is the same as the Waukesha Subdivision, which is made up of manifests, stack container trains, and unit commodity trains. Mainline trains no longer go all the way to North Chicago as they did in Elgin Joliet & Eastern days; however, a local makes a visit there several days a week. Foreign power has become rarer on the "J"; however, with CN's new heritage unit locomotives and various vintage engines hanging on by a thread, trains on the Leithton Subdivision can sometimes have a real treat for locomotive power from the railfan's perspective.

With interlocking towers at Rondout and West Chicago and a restored EJ&E depot in Lake Zurich, there is no shortage of interesting historical locations for photos on the line. The Leithton Subdivision is incredibly important for Canadian National to get trains through the Midwest and is just as important to railfans in Chicagoland.

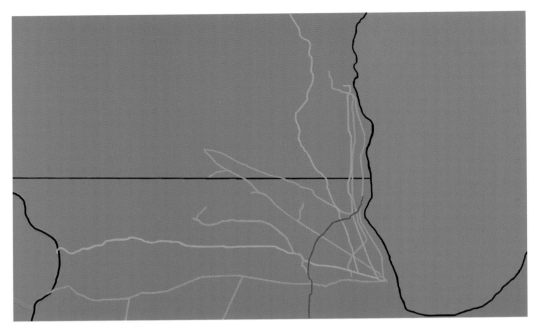

This map of the Canadian National Leithton Subdivision shows the former Elgin Joliet and Eastern making a circle around Chicagoland towards North Chicago where it ends.

A southbound sand train from the summer of 2017 passes JB Tower with a Canadian Pacific EMD SD60 leading with a Kansas City Southern GE AC44CW and a Canadian National GE C40-8W for additional power. As time moves on, trains with a variety of foreign power like this are becoming more and more unusual. [*David Zeman*]

British Columbia Rail 4607, a GE C40-8M, leads a southbound manifest train at Spaulding, the junction between the Canadian National Leithton Subdivision and the Canadian Pacific Elgin Subdivision. [*David Zeman*]

A three pack of Canadian National EMDs, led by SD75I 5714, makes its way south through Hoffman Estates, Illinois heading for CN's Kirk Yard. [*James Keats Jr.*]

BCOL 4652, a GE C44-9W, leads under Route 90 past the siding at Sutton as a mid-winter snow begins the fall. The meeting of two high-priority container trains on the former-Elgin Joliet and Eastern is quite common, as the subdivision is a vital lifeline from Candian National's large yards south of Chicago to Canada. [*James Keats Jr.*]

A specially painted Canadian National ES44AC in "CN 100" paint leads a southbound intermodal train to CN's Joliet Yard. With CN's 100th anniversary, many of their new "GEVOs" got this paint scheme. [*James Keats Jr.*]

British Columbia Rail 4652 leads a southbound stack train through South Barrington to CN's Joliet Yard. This BCOL C44-9W is one of the last of its kind in revenue Canadian National service, but with new PTC systems being implemented, this locomotive will likely never be seen leading in the United States again. [*James Keats Jr.*]

A standard cab Canadian National C40-8 2123 leads a low-priority manifest south to CN's Kirk Yard, shown here at the signal-less signal bridge guarding the UP crossing in Barrington, Illinois. This signal bridge once housed both searchlights and semaphores, but everything has since been removed, and only the masts remain. [*James Keats Jr.*]

One of Canadian National's five heritage units, the Elgin Joliet & Eastern-painted GE ET44AC, leads a northbound stack container train through Lake Zurich, Illinois. Here it crosses the U.S. Rt. 12 bridge which still reads "EJ&E Ry" on the side. [*David Zeman*]

Among many unique locomotives on Canadian National's roster are these Illinois Central "Blue Devil" locomotives. Here we see IC 2460, a GE C40-8W, leading a northbound manifest train past the restored Elgin Joliet & Eastern depot in Lake Zurich, Illinois, in November of 2020. [*David Zeman*]

Since the Elgin Joliet & Eastern was taken over by Canadian National, few trains have regularly gone all the way to the end of the Leithton Subdivision in North Chicago, Illinois. One of the trains that has most recently gone to North Chicago regularly has been CN's local from Schiller Park, Illinois, seen here passing Rondout Tower with two Grand Trunk Western GP9Rs in the summer of 2019 on its return from the end of the line. [*David Zeman*]

6

CANADIAN NATIONAL WAUKESHA SUBDIVISION

Canadian National's Waukesha Subdivision is a highly attractive line for railfans in Chicagoland. With a fair amount of train traffic between mostly freight trains and the occasional Metra commuter train, there is plenty to see. Before being owned by Canadian National, the Wisconsin Central Ltd. ruled the line until 2001 after taking it over from the Soo Line in 1987.

The line starts in Forest Park, Illinois, at the end of the CSX Altenheim Subdivision, and heads north towards Tower B-12, the crossing with the Canadian Pacific Elgin Subdivision, in Franklin Park, IL. While this portion of the line does not see many trains at all, the amount of traffic increases north of B-12 where Metra North Central Service trains turn onto the Waukesha Subdivision and there are more regular freight trains. Just north of B-12 is CN's yard in Schiller Park, which hosts a couple of freight trains per day. Next is Deval, where the Waukesha crosses the Union Pacific Milwaukee Subdivision and the UP Harvard Subdivision in Des Plaines, IL. Franklin Park, Des Plaines, Wheeling, Buffalo Grove, and Mundelein are all suburbs through which the Waukesha Subdivision passes before coming into contact with the CN Leithton Subdivision. When the Waukesha Subdivision and the Leithton Subdivision meet, all freight trains going around the city of Chicago come off the Leithton while facing east and then turn onto the Waukesha to go straight north. The majority of the Waukesha Subdivision's freight traffic comes from down south on the "J," but a couple trains go to/originate from Schiller Park or the inner-city. Metra trains end their journey at Antioch, Illinois, just south of the state line. After crossing the Wisconsin border, the trackage takes trains through Waukesha, Wisconsin where the line crosses the Canadian Pacific Watertown Subdivision at Duplainville. The Wisconsin and Southern Railroad crosses the Waukesha Subdivision in Slinger, WI, and the two lines run parallel for a short time, making for interesting photo opportunities featuring both railroads.

Ten miles south of Fond du Lac is a small town called Byron, WI, which is home to a steep hill, sometimes a problem for heavy southbound freight trains. The end of the line is in Fond du Lac, WI, where the former Wisconsin Central Shops Yard is found. North of there is the CN Neenah Subdivision. Many freight trains can be found using the Waukesha Subdivision every day, averaging between twenty and thirty. Local trains originate out of Fond du Lac, Waukesha, and Schiller Park and these trains are commonly found with older, vintage four-axle locomotives. Uncommon engines from other railroads frequented the line up until late in 2019 when the railroad began to implement Positive Train Control on the line, and since then most trains have been required to have CN engines with PTC installed. Various passenger depots, overpasses, and curves make the line interesting to railroad photographers, and the never-ending train traffic makes the Waukesha Subdivision one of the best lines to see trains in all of Chicago.

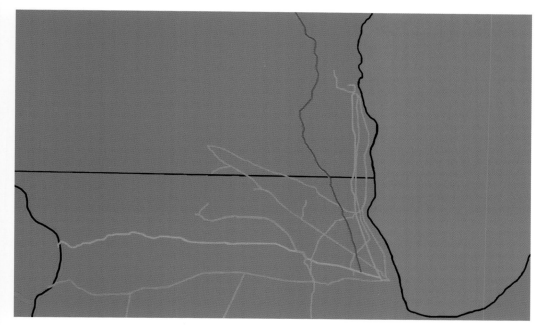

This map of the Canadian National Waukesha Subdivision shows the former Wisconsin Central working its way north into Wisconsin from Chicagoland.

It is very unusual to see a normal freight train with four-axle locomotives for power. In this rare instance, two Grand Trunk Western EMD GP9Rs are in charge of bringing a Potash train from Norpaul Yard into Schiller Park. The two GTW engines were staged out of Schiller Park as the power for the locals from the yard. [*David Zeman*]

A Metra outbound train led by F40PH No. 118 arrives at the Belmont Station, the first stop for Metra on the Waukesha Subdivision, in Franklin Park, Illinois. [*Kyle Krinninger*]

Metra NCS train No. 109 starts off rush hour with a double header of F40PHs, as a storm brews in the background. [*Kyle Krinninger*]

In late 2015, Metra acquired three EMD F59PHs which gave the railroad a bigger variety of power. One of those F59PHs, No. 98, is seen here departing from the Prospect Heights, Illinois, Metra station on a summer day in 2017. [*David Zeman*]

Illinois Central 3107, an EMD GP40R, and Grand Trunk Western 5856, an EMD GP38-2, pull a string of freight cars from industries in Wheeling, Illinois, before bringing their train back to the yard in Schiller Park. This local is known to work out of Schiller Park as far north as Grayslake on weekdays. [*David Zeman*]

Canadian National 2123, a GE C40-8, leads a southbound mixed freight train through Wheeling, Illinois, past the Metra station. These GE C40-8s were initially built for the Chicago and Northwestern Railroad but were later acquired by CN after CNW's merger with the Union Pacific. [*David Zeman*]

Before both Canadian National and Wisconsin Central, the Waukesha Subdivision was owned by the Soo Line. In 2018 and early 2019, CN was leasing many different engines, and here a northbound freight train is passing the station in Wheeling, Illinois, Metra station with one of the leased former-Soo Line EMD SD60s leading the way in a heavy snowstorm. [*David Zeman*]

While the majority of the traffic on the Waukesha Subdivision gets onto the Leithton Subdivision at Mundelein to go around the city of Chicago, a couple of trains a day go straight south and do not get onto the former-EJ&E. This train from Green Bay, Wisconsin, is led by CN 5404, an EMD SD60, and is seen passing the Buffalo Grove, Illinois, Metra station on its way towards Chicago. [*David Zeman*]

An original paint, unpatched Grand Trunk and Western EMD GP9R 4623 with a sister GP9R meets a southbound Metra inbound with an EMD F59PHI at Prairie View, Illinois. While Metra's North Central Service receives very little Metra service, the power on these trains is usually unique. Along with unique Metra power, Canadian National's locals with these GTW GP9Rs is a testament to how unique Chicagoland trains can be. [*James Keats Jr.*]

A southbound rock train going to Mundelein passes through Prairie Crossing in Grayslake, Illinois, with CN 5437, an EMD SD60, leading. These rock trains occur several nights per week on the Waukesha Subdivision and usually run at night. [*David Zeman*]

Canadian National 2341, a GE ES44DC leads three other GEs on a northbound empty tank train at Prairie Crossing. This junction is where the Canadian National Waukesha Subdivision crosses the Metra Fox Lake Subdivision. While it is not a very busy diamond to control on the weekends, during rush hour the constant flow of Metra and freight trains shows how busy this junction can be. [*James Keats Jr.*]

Wisconsin Central returns to its home rails with Canadian National 3069, part of the new "heritage fleet" by CN. This GE ES44AC is leading a potash train all the way down its "home" trackage to Schiller Park, IL, and eventually Gibson, Indiana. [*James Keats Jr.*]

A southbound container stack train rolls past the former Wisconsin Central Waukesha depot with an EMD SD75I at the helm. The depot here at Waukesha, Wisconsin, dates back to the early days of the WC. [*James Keats Jr.*]

A duo of original Illinois Central EMD GP40s lead a southbound local into Duplainville, Wisconsin. Day by day, original paint units on large class ones are disappearing, so this locomotive consist is a true rarity in the area. [*James Keats Jr.*]

Canadian National 5731, a faded red EMD SD75I, rolls south as it approaches the CP diamonds at Duplainville, WI. CN's double stack container trains head all the way down from Canada, and this one is destined for CN's Markham Yard. [*James Keats Jr.*]

In Slinger, Wisconsin, the Wisconsin & Southern can be seen parallel to the Canadian National. Here is a southbound CN train on the Waukesha Subdivision with a GE ES44AC leading passing a WSOR local on their trackage to MIlwaukee. [*David Zeman*]

CN 2855, a GE ES44AC, leads a southbound stack container train through Slinger, Wisconsin. [*David Zeman*]

Candian National 2943, a GE C44-9W, leads a southbound manifest train past a grain elevator in Allenton, Wisconsin. [*James H. Lewnard*]

Canadian National local trains have been known to have some of the most unique locomotives out of any railroad. Here is CN 4100, an EMD GP9RM, and another EMD GP9RM leading a southbound local in Byron, Wisconsin, on August 26th, 2017. Since then, these types of engines have been mostly captive to Canada. [*David Zeman*]

Whenever a freight train is ruled to be too heavy to make it up Byron Hill with only the locomotives on the front of the train, "helper" locomotives are called from the yard in Fond du Lac, Wisconsin, to give the train a shove from the rear as a boost of power. In the spring of 2017, these helper locomotives were Elgin Joliet & Eastern 656, an EMD SD38-2, and Illinois Central 6202, an EMD SD40-3, seen here in Byron, Wisconsin. [*David Zeman*]

Canadian National 8879, an EMD SD70M-2, leads a southbound manifest train down the Waukesha Subdivision at County Rd. B in Byron, Wisconsin. [*David Zeman*]

7

CANADIAN PACIFIC
C&M SUBDIVISION

The Canadian Pacific C&M (Chicago & Milwaukee) Subdivision is one of the most popular subdivisions for railfans to watch trains. It was previously owned by the Soo Line Railroad who took over the Milwaukee Road in 1987, and Canadian Pacific took control of the trackage in 1990. As one part of Canadian Pacific's main artery to the Twin Cities, there is a lot of train traffic that can bring a variety of different types of trains. The line starts in Chicago Union Station where Amtrak and Metra trains for the C&M and several other lines originate. Metra timetables refer to the C&M Subdivision routing as the "Milwaukee District North"; however, trains on the MDN do not terminate on the C&M. Trains on Metra's Milwaukee District West, Milwaukee District North, and North Central Service lines leave Chicago Union Station and use the C&M for several miles. At Tower A-2, the C&M crosses the Union Pacific Geneva Subdivision, creating one of the most high-trafficked junctions for trains in the entire country. Further up the line at Tower A-5, the Canadian Pacific Elgin Subdivision begins. A-5 (5 miles from Chicago) is where Metra trains bound for the MDW and NCS lines turn left onto the Elgin Subdivision. After crossing the Union Pacific Harvard Subdivision at Mayfair, the C&M Subdivision runs through Chicago suburbs such as Edgebrook, Morton Grove, Glenview, Northbrook, and Lake Forest. At Rondout, the line crosses the Canadian National Leithton Subdivision, and the Metra Fox Lake Subdivision begins as it splits west from the CP. Metra MDN trains continue onto the Fox Lake Subdivision and terminate at the station in Fox Lake, Illinois, leaving Amtrak as the only passenger trains north of Rondout.

Being one of the last locations in the Midwest with both an interlocking tower and searchlight signals guarding the junction, Rondout is one of the most popular railfanning locations in Chicago. Moving north on the C&M, the line ends up north of the Wisconsin border in towns such as Kenosha and Sturtevant. Finally, the C&M Subdivision ends after passing through the Amtrak station in downtown Milwaukee, Wisconsin, at Milepost 87.1, which is also the west end of CP's Muskego Yard. Some of the Amtrak trains from Chicago make their last stop at the station in Milwaukee, while some continue west through the Twin Cities to the West Coast. The freight traffic on the C&M Subdivision travels between St. Paul, Minnesota, and Chicago. Most of the freight trains are mixed manifests and stack trains, but unit bulk trains such as grain trains and oil trains are also very common. The majority of freight trains of all types get on the C&M to go north at Tower A-20, the over-under crossing with the Union Pacific Milwaukee Subdivision, but some freights get onto the line at A-5 after traveling on the Elgin Subdivision.

Most of the locomotives used on freight trains are Canadian Pacific engines, but foreign power is also common. This Subdivision has been known to host all sorts of abnormal train movements, locomotives, and excursions including steam engines, Mexican locomotives, and work trains. The line is littered with photogenic spots filled with history for railfans, including the aforementioned Rondout Tower, Sturtevant searchlight signals, Deerfield train depot, and many more. With lots of different trains and plenty of interesting locations at which one can watch them, the C&M Subdivision is one of the staple lines for railfanning in Chicagoland.

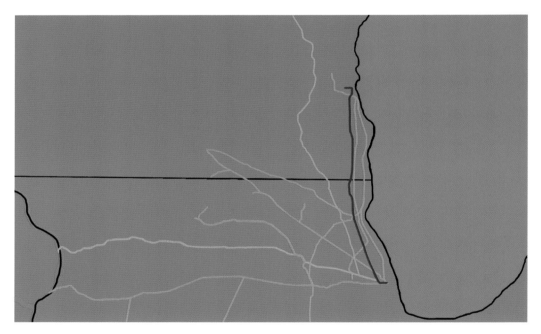

This map of the Canadian Pacific C&M Subdivision shows the former Milwaukee Road working its way North into Milwaukee from Chicago.

Opposite page

Above: Downtown Chicago holds many interesting and unique spots to railfans. Here is Amtrak No. 8, the inbound Empire Builder at the East end of CP Morgan. This signal bridge spots a whopping six searchlight signals, from back in the days of the Milwaukee Road. [*James Keats Jr.*]

Below: Metra EMD F40PH No. 124 leads an outbound Milwaukee District train at CP Morgan in Chicago, Illinois. [*David Zeman*]

With its famed Pennsylvania Railroad position lights still atop the signal bridge, AMTK 504, a very unique GE B32-8WH, shoves a Hiawatha Service train under the west end of CP Morgan. These signals have since been replaced by newer LED lights, ending an era of these massive position lights being prevalent in Chicago. [*James Keats Jr.*]

One of Amtrak's premier trains, the Empire Builder, departs Chicago on a rather gloomy day with three GE P42DCs (including one of Amtrak's heritage engines). This train is rolling past Tower A-2, a manned tower that has controlled one of the busiest areas in all of Chicagoland since the days of the Milwaukee Road. [*James Keats Jr.*]

METX 413, an MPI MP36PH-3S, brings an outbound Milwaukee District train past Tower A-2 at Western Avenue in Chicago, Illinois. This spot is one of the most highly trafficked interlockings in Chicago and the entire country, as it sees trains from Metra's Milwaukee District North and West Lines, Metra's North Central Service, and Metra's Union Pacific West Line. [*David Zeman*]

Just after passing Western Avenue Coach Yard, an inbound Milwaukee District train arrives at the Western Ave. Metra Station as it passes through interlocking at A-3. [*David Zeman*]

Metra's Western Avenue Coach Yard serves as the epicenter of commuter rail action north and west of Chicago Union Station. This bird's eye view has a little bit of everything: all of Metra's operating locomotive types, brand-new rail cars under wraps, and even a one-off paint scheme, all in the shadow of the Windy City's iconic skyline. [*David Dupuis*]

Nickel Plate Road 765 (Lima 2-8-4 Berkshire) leads "The Varsity" excursion train to Janesville, WI, seen on an early morning in Morton Grove, IL, in June of 2016. [*Kyle Krinninger*]

WAMX 4192, an EMD SD40-2, leads a rare daylight Wisconsin and Southern Railroad grain train through Northbrook, Illinois, at Tower A-20. WSOR trains on the C&M Subdivision usually run at night, and the searchlights signals pictured in this photo were replaced in early 2017. [*David Zeman*]

Soo Line No. 6027, an EMD SD60, leads an eastbound freight train onto the connection at Tower A-20 which would take this train to the Union Pacific Milwaukee Subdivision. The searchlight signals on the left were replaced shortly thereafter, and the Soo Line engine was repainted into Canadian Pacific's paint scheme. [*David Zeman*]

A Canadian Pacific GE ES44AC leads a southbound manifest train past the Northbrook Metra station. [*Kyle Krinninger*]

After roughly 2015, it was very uncommon for one of CP's intermodal trains to or from Canada to have anything but a GE locomotive. This very unusual CP intermodal train has CP 6068, an EMD SD40-2, and another SD40-2 for power after the third engine, a CP AC44CW, stopped working in Wisconsin. The train is seen here passing the historic former-Milwaukee Road passenger station in Deerfield, Illinois. [*David Zeman*]

A southbound Amtrak Hiawatha train bound for Chicago passes through Rondout, Illinois, with an Amtrak GE B32-WH leading. These B32-8WH locomotives are typically used when there is a problem with the regular locomotive on these trains, and that was just the case here as the Siemens SC-44 engine on the other end of the train had experienced issues. [*David Zeman*]

It is common for Metra trains to have two locomotives for power. In this case, an outbound Milwaukee District North train passes Rondout Tower with METX 123, an EMD F40PH, leading a former-Amtrak EMD F59PHI. [*David Zeman*]

Canadian Pacific 5922, an EMD SD40-2, and another SD40-2 lead a northbound rail train past Rondout Tower in the last moments of daylight in January of 2019. [*David Zeman*]

Soo Line No. 1003, an Alco 2-8-2 "Mikado," passes Rondout Tower while heading back to its home in Hartford, Wisconsin, after running to Chicago for a charity event in the summer of 2017. [*David Zeman*]

When the Milwaukee Road was bought up and went out of business, many commuter engineers stayed with Metra for work on the lines they already knew so well. Here's Metra 405, the Milwaukee Road heritage MPI MP36PH, taking the last Milwaukee Road engineer on his retirement run through Rondout, passing the Milwaukee Road tower. [*James Keats Jr.*]

Amtrak 90200, a freshly repainted Amtrak "Non-Powered Control Unit" or NPCU, rolls south through the interlocking at Rondout to Chicago on Amtrak's Hiawatha Service. This NPCU unit was once an F40PH but has since had its traction motors removed and is now used as space for baggage, explaining the large door on the side. [*James Keats Jr.*]

With Lake effect snow starting to fall, Norfolk Southern 1070, an EMD SD70ACe, leads a northbound manifest freight under the north end of Rondout. Foreign power is already very common on Canadian Pacific manifest trains, but this Wabash heritage unit was quite the treat! [*James Keats Jr.*]

Amtrak NPCU 90222 leads train 332, a southbound Hiawatha service, splitting the searchlights at Sturtevant, Wisconsin, on a late July morning. [*James H. Lewnard*]

With the fall foliage putting out a strong showing, the Amtrak Empire Builder makes its way south with AMTK 68, a GE P42DC. Track speed for the Amtrak trains is quite fast in southern Wisconsin, this one doing 70 MPH approaching Caledonia, WI. [*James Keats Jr.*]

North of the border, many of the original pole lines from the Milwaukee Road days still remain lining the tracks. Here is CP 9765, a GE AC44CW, making its way south through the small town of Caledonia, Wisconsin. [*James Keats Jr.*]

The occasional Canadian Pacific business train usually brings a long passenger train led by a set of "F" units. This business train was slightly out of the ordinary, as it is powered by CP 1401, an EMD FP9A, and another EMD FP9A sandwiching a red Canadian Pacific GP20C-ECO. Here, the train is leaving Milwaukee, Wisconsin, as it passes through the interlocking at KK on a nice May morning in 2019. [*David Zeman*]

The occasional ballast train can bring interesting locomotives with it. This ballast train, powered by two Canadian Pacific EMD SD40-2s, goes through the interlocking at KK in Milwaukee, Wisconsin, in the spring of 2020. [*David Zeman*]

The Canadian Pacific Holiday Train arrives in Milwaukee, Wisconsin, as it crosses the Menomonee River before holding an event at the Amtrak station. [*David Zeman*]

The annual Canadian Pacific Holiday Train sits in the Amtrak station in Milwaukee, Wisconsin, in December of 2017. The train had come from Chicago earlier that same day and was to spend the night in CP's Muskego Yard in Milwaukee before going further west the next day. [*David Zeman*]

CP AC44CW No. 9732 leads a westbound intermodal train through Duplainville, Wisconsin, at the CN diamonds. This crossing is where the Canadian Pacific crosses the Canadian National Waukesha Subdivision, and the CP signals protecting the junction are still searchlights. Duplainville is technically on the CP Watertown Subdivision, but is worth noting because of the junction with the Waukesha Subdivision at this location. [*David Zeman*]

8

WISCONSIN SOUTHERN AND METRA FOX LAKE SUBDIVISIONS

The Metra Fox Lake Branch takes a hard left off the Canadian Pacific C&M Subdivision to the far north suburbs of Illinois. The Subdivision offers a good balance of decent trains and good shots. Starting at Rondout, the Fox Lake Subdivision runs northwest through towns such as Libertyville, Grayslake, Long Lake, and Fox Lake. This branch off the main Canadian Pacific lifeline to Canada offers a good example of suburban railfanning. As Metra winds its way through the small towns near the Wisconsin border, many attractive curve shots are at hand for any railfan willing to make the drive north. The close proximity to northern Illinois "Chain-O-Lakes" offers some unique shots as well, as trains often roll though lakeside trackage.

Once Metra reaches Fox Lake, service ends and the trackage takes new ownership by the Wisconsin and Southern Railroad. The WSOR operates mostly in Wisconsin, but its dip south from Janesville, WI, into Illinois showcases a great Class 2 operation. Rolling through small towns such as Avalon, Zenda, Walworth, and Spring Grove, the WSOR runs nightly trains down Metra trackage to the large Belt Railway of Chicago Clearing Yard. The Wisconsin shortline offers a true treat to anyone willing to stay up near midnight, as their roster is filled with vintage EMD SD40s.

Shown throughout this chapter is WSOR's various trains north and south of the state line, as well as the usual and rare Metra daily moves. Speaking of rarities, the Fox Lake Subdivision also has had its fair share of steam excursions. Both the Nickel Plate 765 and the Soo Line 1003 have traversed the Subdivision. With the Fox Lake branch only being a single track mainline with passing sidings, not a whole lot of action is to be had during the weekends or in the middle of weekdays, but just like any other Metra route, rush hour is a true sight to behold. As Metra and WSOR come together, they symbolize a great example of single-track railroading, and the frequent freight and passenger trains alike make this subdivision truly worthwhile. The Fox Lake Subdivision deserves its recognition and documentation as one of the most interesting Chicagoland routes.

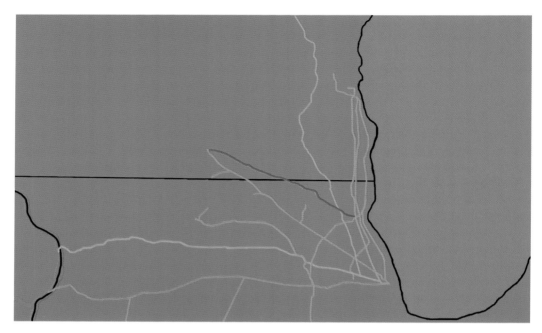

This map of the Metra and Wisconsin and Southern Fox Lake Subdivision shows the former Milwaukee Road working its way West into Wisconsin from Rondout.

At the very start of the Fox Lake Subdivision, Metra MP36PH No. 414 splits the Northern searchlights at Rondout, just outside Libertyville. With constant talks of these searchlight signals being replaced, many railfans are getting their shots in preparation for a total signal replacement. [*James Keats Jr.*]

Metra F59PHI No. 73 leads an outbound train for Fox Lake over the Des Plaines River in Libertyville, Illinois. The Amtrak Pacific Surfliner paint scheme that this F59PHI wears is rather out of place on this frigid night. [*David Dupuis*]

Metra MP36PH 414 finds itself shoving an inbound train to Chicago past Metra's newest depot on the Fox Lake Subdivision, Libertyville. This station has a very unique classic look to it, with a modern touch essential to all new stations. This new depot has to be one of the best in the Northern Suburbs. [*James Keats Jr.*]

The nightly westbound Wisconsin and Southern freight train passes the Prairie Crossing passenger station in Grayslake, Illinois, with WAMX 4171, an EMD SD40-2, on the point. [*David Zeman*]

Nickel Plate Road 765 (Lima 2-8-4 Berkshire) leads "The Varsity" excursion train eastbound through Grayslake, IL, on its way back to Glenview, IL, in the summer of 2016. [*Kyle Krinninger*]

A Metra Nippon-Sharyo cab car leads an inbound train at track speed through Long Lake, IL. This inbound is speeding by the railroad's form of a speed limit sign—as the train passes this sign, it can increase its speed to 55 miles-per-hour, but for a train going the other way, it must slow to 35. Fifty-five is the maximum speed trains can go on all of the Fox Lake branch. [*James Keats Jr.*]

An inbound Metra train being shoved by MPI MP36PH No. 404, works its way past the frozen Long Lake in Long Lake, Illinois. The rather short train featured in this picture is as a result of COVID-19. Metra has deemed five cars the perfect social distance train size for its weekend trains. [*James Keats Jr.*]

Two commemorative Metra MP36PHs rest out the weekend at the Fox Lake, IL, coach yard, one being METX 405 for the Milwaukee Road, and the other being METX 401, a dedication unit to a young cancer victim, who absolutely loved Metra before his untimely passing. [*James Keats Jr.*]

Metra F40PH-3 No. 115 reaches the end of the line for commuter service in Fox Lake, Illinois. Just behind this shot is northern Illinois' popular "Chain-O-Lakes." [*James Keats Jr.*]

Soo Line 1003 (Alco 2-8-2 "Mikado") heads west through Fox Lake after a run to Chicago on a summer morning in 2017. [*David Zeman*]

Wisconsin and Southern EMD SD40-2 No. 4170 works its way through Zenda, WI, on a late, cold winter night. The sign to the right of 4170 sports a Milwaukee Road herald, alluding to the Milwaukee Road Historical Society. The plaque also shown in the shot dedicates the sign to a local Milwaukee Road fan, who has since passed away. [*James Keats Jr.*]

In a scene that shows the Wisconsin and Southern Railroad at its finest, WAMX 4170, WSOR's commemorative fortieth anniversary SD40-2, works a grain elevator in Zenda, Wisconsin. [*James Keats Jr.*]

9

UNION PACIFIC MILWAUKEE SUBDIVISION

Union Pacific has two different ways to get to Milwaukee, Wisconsin, from Chicago. The main route for freight trains to travel between the two locations is on the UP Milwaukee Subdivision. Like the other UP lines mentioned, the line was acquired by the Union Pacific in 1995 after taking over the CNW. Starting at Proviso Yard, the Milwaukee Subdivision, also referred to as the Chicago and Northwestern's "New Line," crosses over Canadian Pacific's Bensenville Yard just south of O'Hare Airport. At Bryn Mawr, just north of Bensenville Yard, the CP's connection track joins with the UP. North of there, Canadian Pacific uses the Milwaukee Subdivision as an alternate route to access the C&M Subdivision to Milwaukee. In Des Plaines, Illinois, the "New Line" crosses the UP Harvard Subdivision and the Canadian National Waukesha Subdivision at Deval in Des Plaines, IL. From there north, any Canadian Pacific run-through trains get off the Milwaukee Subdivision at Shermer in Northbrook, IL, and get onto the C&M Subdivision. Union Pacific trains continue north through suburbs such as Lake Forest, Lake Bluff, and North Chicago. A number of trains, such as coal trains for power plants along Lake Michigan, utilize a connection in Lake Bluff, IL, to get from the Milwaukee Subdivision to the UP Kenosha Subdivision as an alternate routing towards Milwaukee. While the two routes run parallel to one another north along the Lake, the Milwaukee Subdivision remains a few miles further inland. The two subdivisions finally converge at St. Francis in Milwaukee, and from there the trackage curves to the west around the city before heading straight north to Butler Yard. At the north end of the Yard, the Milwaukee Subdivision trackage ends.

Traffic on the Milwaukee Subdivision is exclusively freight trains, except for the occasional business train. Coal trains, manifest trains, locals, and other unit trains are most commonly seen. The "New Line" lacks the photogenic locations in some respects compared to other railroad lines around Chicago, but there are still enough historical locations and favorite railfanning spots for photographers to enjoy, from searchlights to special curve shots. From the most common freight trains to the unusual steam locomotive excursion, the Union Pacific Milwaukee Subdivision deserves coverage and recognition for its variety of interesting trains.

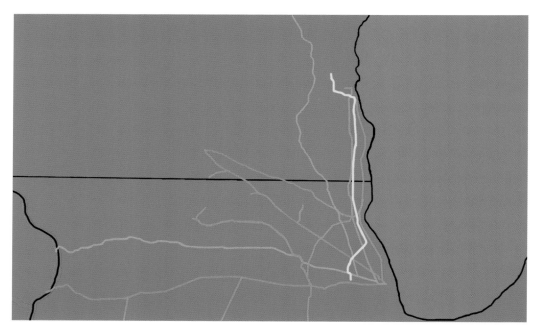

This map of the Union Pacific Milwaukee Subdivision shows the newer routing for trains to get to Milwaukee from Chicago.

Canadian Pacific 6230, an EMD SD60, and a Union Pacific SD70M, power a southbound train through Des Plaines, Illinois, at Howard Avenue. [*David Zeman*]

Still sporting its original Cotton Belt paint, Union Pacific 1158, an EMD GP60, takes a southbound local to Proviso Yard at the Howard Avenue curve, a popular railfanning location in Chicagoland. [*James Keats Jr.*]

A northbound coal train, left, led by a Union Pacific GE AC45CCTE, meets a local train, right, working an industry with an EMD GP38-2 and an EMD GP15-1 in Des Plaines, Illinois. [*David Zeman*]

Union Pacific 1948, EMD SD40N, leads a southbound coal train in Des Plaines, Illinois. The SD40N was needed as a pilot locomotive due to cab signaling requirements on the Kenosha Subdivision. [*David Zeman*]

Two Canadian Pacific EMD SD40-2s exercise CP's trackage rights on the Union Pacific while taking a northbound welded rail train towards the C&M Subdivision as they cross the UP Harvard Subdivision at Deval. [*David Zeman*]

Canadian Pacific EMD SD60 No. 6303 and a Union Pacific EMD SD70AH lead a southbound manifest freight through Deval. Deval is a large interlocking in Des Plaines, Illinois, with diamonds on a wooden trestle directly over Illinois Rt. 14. With three different railroad lines crossing each other at Deval, the junction can see well over seventy trains per day. [*James Keats Jr.*]

Five Union Pacific EMD four-axle locomotives, including a former-Cotton Belt GP60, bring a southbound local into Des Plaines, Illinois. This train came from Waukegan, Illinois, and ended up dropping parts of its train in Proviso and Des Plaines. [*David Zeman*]

Left: Union Pacific Big Boy 4014, the largest locomotive ever produced, is seen working its way south on the Milwaukee Subdivision, with a large plume of black smoke. From this bridge, over thirty photographers captured 4014 rolling into Northbrook, Illinois. [*James Keats Jr.*]

Below: Union Pacific EMD SD70ACe No. 1989, the Denver & Rio Grande Western heritage unit, leads a southbound coal train past the signals through the interlocking at Valley on the Milwaukee Subdivision in Northbrook, Illinois. [*David Zeman*]

Union Pacific 1111, an EMD SD70ACe dedicated to honor the employees of the railroad, leads a southbound business train through Kenosha, Wisconsin, on the Milwaukee Subdivision. [*David Zeman*]

With surroundings full of fall colors, Union Pacific 9034, an EMD SD70AH, leads a southbound Manifest through Caledonia, Wisconsin. This train is over 10,000 feet long and bound for UP's Proviso Yard. [*James Keats Jr.*]

10

UNION PACIFIC KENOSHA SUBDIVISION

The Kenosha Subdivision was the Chicago & Northwestern Railroad's original pathway to Milwaukee from Chicago. Owned by the Union Pacific since its merger with the CNW in 1995, this line travels close to Lake Michigan and hosts mostly Metra trains closer to Chicago and some freight trains north of Kenosha, Wisconsin. The trackage of the Kenosha Subdivision begins in Chicago at Clybourn, just before the Metra station that resides there. Metra trains bound for the Kenosha Subdivision, referred to by Metra as the Union Pacific North Line, use the Geneva Subdivision and then the Harvard Subdivision before splitting off at Clybourn. The line then travels through the neighborhoods on the north side of Chicago before hitting suburbs such as Evanston, Wilmette, Lake Forest, and Waukegan. Lake Bluff sees a connection with the Milwaukee Subdivision called the Lake Subdivision, and it is used by coal trains or local trains needing access to the Kenosha Subdivision along the Lake. Metra trains terminate in Kenosha, WI, and the line north of there is strictly freight traffic. In the stretch of trackage between Kenosha and Milwaukee, the Oak Creek power plant, which receives coal trains from UP, awaits its last cut of cars before converting to pipeline gas in the coming years. Several other industries receive different types of railcars from UP on the Kenosha Subdivision.

Finally, the end of the line is at St. Francis in Milwaukee where the trackage becomes the Milwaukee Subdivision until Butler Yard outside of Milwaukee. As previously said, the line south of Kenosha sees mostly Metra trains but is not unfamiliar to an occasional work train or other run-through trains north of Lake Bluff. Coal trains, manifests, and other unit trains can use the Kenosha Subdivision north of the Lake Subdivision connection. The northern suburbs of Chicago boast several impressive Metra stations, among other great locations for photos including Clybourn, Racine, and many more. The UP Kenosha Subdivision, while being one of the least-recognized subdivisions among railfans, is an important part to railroading in Chicagoland.

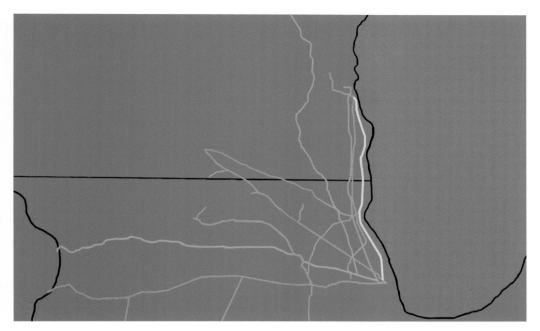

This map of the Union Pacific Kenosha Subdivision, and its branch line at Kenosha, Wisconsin, show the former Chicago and Northwestern working its way North into Wisconsin from Chicago.

Metra 140, an EMD F40PH, takes an outbound passenger train on the Kenosha Subdivision bound for Kenosha, Wisconsin. This is unlike any other Metra train because of the former Chicago and Northwestern passenger car that rides between the locomotive and the rest of the train. This private piece of equipment rode from Kenosha in the morning to Chicago and back to Kenosha in the evening on weekdays until the start of the 2020 COVID-19 pandemic. [*David Zeman*]

With a backdrop of Chicago's skyline, Metra F40PH-2 160 shoves an inbound train into the city while passing over an old Chicago and Northwestern lift bridge. [*James Keats Jr.*]

Metra 126, an EMD F40PH, makes a stop at the Ravenswood passenger station on the north side of Chicago, Illinois. [*David Zeman*]

On the southern part of the Kenosha Subdivision, revenue freight trains have not been seen in several decades, so the only way to see freight locomotives are on work trains. Union Pacific Y715, an EMD GP15AC, is seen here leading a southbound ballast train through Rogers Park in Chicago, Illinois, bound for Ravenswood, where the ballast would be dropped. [*David Zeman*]

There are a variety of nice passenger depots on the Kenosha Subdivision for Metra riders to enjoy. One of these depots is in Kenilworth, Illinois, seen here being passed by a Metra EMD F40PH pulling an outbound express commuter train. [*David Zeman*]

Metra 90, the EMD F59PHI in Chicago & Northwestern livery, powers an outbound commuter train as it arrives in Winnetka, Illinois. [*David Zeman*]

Union Pacific Y723, an EMD GP15-1, brings a disabled Metra set south through Glencoe, Illinois, during a very snowy day. These yard locomotives are typically seen bringing singular bad-ordered rail cars between downtown terminals and suburban coach yards—seeing them on the point of a full passenger set is somewhat of a rarity. [*David Dupuis*]

Union Pacific 1173, an EMD GP60, pulls a Butler-based local train through Kenosha, Wisconsin, on UP's Farm Subdivision. This line is one of a few fragments of the old Kenosha Division line that are still in operation. [*David Dupuis*]

Union Pacific 1173 stands by in Kenosha, Wisconsin, with a Butler-based local train. This station is the end of the line for Metra's Union Pacific North Line, although only a fraction of scheduled trains make it this far. To the photographer's left is a wye that leads down to Kenosha's small coach yard, as well as the UP Farm Subdivision. [*David Dupuis*]

Union Pacific 1158 again, working its way south out of Racine with a loaded rock train to Waukegan. 1158 has been a resident of the Chicagoland area for roughly the past year, and it is by far the most popular unit to catch on local trains in the north suburbs. [*James Keats Jr.*]

Union Pacific 1158, an EMD GP60 still sporting its Cotton Belt paint, works its way south through Racine, Wisconsin and over the old Chicago and Northwestern swing bridge spanning the Root River. [*James Keats Jr.*]

11

ILLINOIS RAILWAY MUSEUM

The Illinois Railway Museum is a not-for-profit organization powered by hundreds of volunteers and it is the largest railroad museum in the United States. Founded in the early 1950s, the museum started with the purchase of one train car. Seventy years later, there are hundreds more trains to see. As a home to over 500 pieces of railroad equipment from steam engines to freight cars, the IRM has a 5-mile mainline for visitors to enjoy. The museum brings in thousands of visitors every year from young children who love trains to the older generation who may remember seeing vintage cars running when they were younger.

Several special events are held on weekends of the summer months at IRM, including the "Museum Showcase," which features the museum's most unique equipment in operation, or the "Diesel Days" event, a weekend dedicated to running exclusively diesel locomotives. On occasion, a special day dedicated to photographers is set aside to put on daytime and nighttime displays for amazing pictures.

Plenty of the trains at the museum are incredibly unique or are the last of their kind, including the Chicago Burlington & Quincy 9911A, the last EMD E5 in existence. The museum's 2-10-0 Russian "Decapod" locomotive, the Frisco 1630, is the only one of its kind that is still operable, and the Chicago Rock Island & Pacific 4506 is the only EMD GP7R left in CRIP paint. Other favorites to many people at the museum are the Nebraska Zephyr, the coach train, the electric interurban trains, and the trolleys.

There is something for everyone to enjoy at the museum, and the volunteers that keep it moving work endlessly to bring new opportunities to experience every year for visitors and railfans. The trains and exhibits live inside the minds of the people who visit. Unforgettable trains and wonderful volunteers to keep the museum moving make it truly an amazing place for railfans or anyone else to experience.

Both of the Museum's currently operable steam locomotives, J. Neil Lumber Co. 5 (Lima Shay) and St. Louis-San Francisco Railway 1630 (Baldwin 2-10-0), bring the coach train onto the museum mainline at the "East Switch." [*David Zeman*]

Two vintage Chicago Transit Authority "L" cars are seen on the museum's "West Wye" next to the 50th Ave. elevated platform. [*David Zeman*]

Chicago & Northwestern 4160, an EMD GP7, pushes a demonstration freight train westbound on the Museum's mainline past the semaphore signals at Olson Rd. This engine was restored and repainted in 2018 to wear Rock Island paint as CRIP 4506. [*David Zeman*]

Metra 308 and Chicago and Northwestern 411, both EMD F7s, rest on IRM's wye track next to the restored Santa Fe lighted sign which once sat atop the Railway Exchange Building in downtown Chicago. [*James Keats Jr.*]

Rock Island 4506 and Illinois Terminal 1605, both EMD GP7s, speed past a mail bag set up for a Railway Post Office demonstration. Every showcase weekend, IRM puts on wonderful demonstrations showing the mail catch on the fly. [*James Keats Jr.*]

The famous CBQ 9911-A "Silver Pilot" EMD E5A and its Nebraska Zephyr train set roll east at Johnson Siding. This run was an after-hours special with members of the museum and volunteers alike enjoying the evening sunset. [*James Keats Jr.*]

Green Bay & Western 2407, an Alco RSD15, departs from the museum's main depot with a coach train during a "Diesel Days" event. [*David Zeman*]

Southern Pacific 1518, IRM's resident EMD SD7 (which was also the first ever SD7) works its way past my family's 1970 Chevrolet Chevelle. Both of these vintage GM products dominated the rails and the road decades ago. [*James Keats Jr.*]

For special events such as the museum's "Showcase Weekend," volunteers sometimes stage photo lineups featuring unique locomotives. This lineup features, from left to right, Chicago Burlington & Quincy 504 (EMD SD24), Chicago Rock Island & Pacific 4506 (EMD GP7), Atchison Topeka & Santa Fe 92 (EMD FP45), and Chicago Burlington & Quincy 9255 (EMD SW7). [*David Zeman*]

Opposite page

Above: At this once-in-a-lifetime event at the museum, a reunion of various pieces of Chicago and Northwestern equipment gathered for a nighttime photo session. In this lineup, from left to right: CNW 151 (Pullman Bilevel Cab Car), CNW 1689 (Alco RSD-5), CNW 6847 (EMD SD40-2), CNW 8701 (GE C44-9W), and CNW 8646 (GE C44-9W). [*David Zeman*]

Below: Chicago and Northwestern 411, an EMD F7A, brings the CNW bilevel commuter train westbound past position signals on the museum's mainline during the "Diesel Days" event. [*David Zeman*]

12

MISCELLANEOUS TRAINS & RAILROAD OPERATIONS

Chicagoland has always been known for the hustle and bustle of its large Class I railroads. These railroads connect Chicago's industries to the world market and keep America moving. With Chicago being such a big city, and having numerous suburbs around it, the Class I giants simply cannot handle all the small switching and interchange operations in small towns and big cities alike. This chapter highlights all these unspoken operations. The short lines and regional railroads of the Midwest make up a small, but extremely important aspect of modern-day railroading. Anything in Chicago that doesn't fit under a large Class I umbrella sits here, in "Miscellaneous." From streetcars to storage, from short lines to grain elevator switchers, the trains that are not in a museum or are on a Class I find a home here. With the numerous small businesses and industrial parks in Chicago and its suburbs, there is quite a bit to see. The diversity of Chicagoland is shown in its large railroads, but expanded upon greatly in these photos, showing the unspoken base to the large industry of railroading. Chicago's shortlines, stored equipment, small passenger operations, and interchanging railroads make up the heart of small-town operations and help the Midwest continue moving. These are the unsung heroes of railroading.

Opposite page

Above: ILSX 921, an EMD SW1500, brings a cut of cars from the industrial park in Bensenville, Illinois, into the Canadian Pacific yard in Bensenville in the summer of 2018. This operation which switched cars between the CP and industries in Bensenville was owned by Iowa Pacific Holdings until 2019 when Progress Rail took over. [*David Zeman*]

Below: In early 2017, Iowa Pacific's "Hoosier State" train from Chicago to Indianapolis stopped their operations, and the equipment from the trains ended up in several locations around the country. Some pieces of that equipment landed in the industrial park in Bensenville, Illinois, including this Iowa Pacific EMD GP40FH-2 No. 4137 photographed at night with two CEFX EMD GP20Ds. [*David Zeman*]

An abandoned former Chicago Burlington & Quincy, Burlington Northern, MARC, and Iowa Pacific EMD E9 sits accompanied by Chicago O'Hare traffic in Bensenville. [*James Keats Jr.*]

ILSX 942, a former Southern Pacific EMD MP15, leads Progressive Rail's Bensenville south job under the half built Illinois Route 390 in Elk Grove Village. [*James Keats Jr.*]

Progressive Rail keeps their power diverse and eye-catching, shown here with a former CP EMD GP9 1507. The banners that adorn the side handrails are an excellent marketing strategy to show the effectiveness of railroads. [*James Keats Jr.*]

With Illinois' third biggest city, Rockford, putting out industrial products, plant switchers are needed to move around the commodities. Here, a vintage GE center-cab locomotive switches out scrap steel just outside downtown Rockford. [*James Keats Jr.*]

Traversing the old CNW "KD" line, TDCX 202, a seventy-year-old plant switcher for Chemung, Illinois' DeLong Grain works its way west on the main. 202 is hauling over 100 grain cars all by itself in this photo. [*James Keats Jr.*]

Just west of Harvard, Illinois, sits Chemung, Illinois, a small town generated around the large DeLong Company grain elevator. The grain elevator's SW7 is shown here with the UP road power off to the side. [*James Keats Jr.*]

TDCX 202, an EMD SW7, brings a cut of empty grain cars towards the facility in Chemung, Illinois, where the cars will be loaded for the Union Pacific. [*David Zeman*]

Kenosha, Wisconsin has a very unique trolley loop that runs down the middle of the streets in downtown and along Lake Michigan. Pictured here is TTC 4549, a Toronto Transit PCC Street Car built by Saint Louis Car, running towards the lake down 56th Street. [*David Zeman*]

ABOUT THE AUTHORS

MR. JAMES KEATS JR. is a thriving photographer from Chicagoland's far northwestern suburbs in Illinois. Growing up in the region of the former Chicago and Northwestern was no easy task, as many relics from the former railroad giant remain in the region. Using modern day social media platforms, Keats shares his view on Chicago and the Midwest as a whole, with shots ranging from Northern Wisconsin to Southern Indiana and Central Iowa. Living near the Illinois Railway Museum, the largest rail museum in the country, as well as Interstate 90 directly to Chicago, Keats' large collection documents the modern Chicagoland rail scene at its very best.

DAVID ZEMAN is a college-age photographer from the northwest suburbs of Chicago. Inspired by many older photographers of trains, he grew a passion for documenting railroads on camera as a teenager. By making use of social media and having a large network of friends, Zeman has been able to take photos of the ever-changing railroad scene around Chicagoland. While having broad interest in the railroads, he has a target of finding and photographing trains that he finds exceptionally interesting. From the western suburbs of Chicago to southeastern Wisconsin, he shares his best photos from locations spread out throughout the region.